# SUGAR
# FREE

CLB 2436
© 1991 Colour Library Books Ltd, Godalming, Surrey, England
All rights reserved
This edition published in 1991 by Gallery Books,
an imprint of W.H. Smith Publishers, Inc.,
112 Madison Avenue, New York 10016
Printed and bound in Singapore
ISBN 0 8317 8048 7

Gallery Books are available for bulk purchase for sales promotions
and premium use. For details write or telephone
the Manager of Special Sales, W.H. Smith Publishers, Inc.,
112 Madison Avenue, New York, New York 10016 (212) 532-6600.

GALLERY BOOKS

# Introduction

In today's health-conscious atmosphere we are all becoming more aware of the disadvantages of a high sugar intake – increasing levels of obesity and tooth decay are the most obvious results of just such a diet. We now eat as much sugar in two weeks as people of two centuries ago did in one year, yet as we live less active lives, we actually require less energy than our forefathers.

There are many misconceptions about the properties of sugar. Contrary to what many people believe, sugar does not contain any nutrients and all types of sugar, whether white or brown, or in the form of honey or maple syrup, have the same calorific value. Sugar, or sucrose to give it its technical name, is a complex carbohydrate made up of two simple sugars. The first, fructose, is the sweetest and is found naturally in fruits. The second, glucose, is formed by the body during the digestion of plants and vegetables. Sugars are all digested in the same way: the sugar is broken down into glucose, which then travels around in the blood as energy; if this energy isn't used, it is stored as fat reserves.

By eating naturally sweet foods we can educate our palates to prefer these to over-sweet, sugared foods. The extra chewing needed will also produce more saliva to clean away the sugary film from the teeth and help prevent decay. As naturally sweet foods also take longer to digest, our bodies will not experience the short-lived artificial "highs" that refined sugars produce.

Unfortunately, it is not always possible to leave sugar out of recipes as it can be vital for a dish's preservation or structure. However, cutting down our sugar intake gradually and avoiding those processed foods which contain sugar is a big step towards a more healthful diet. In addition, eating more naturally sweet foods containing fructose, such as strawberries, not only reduces calorie intake but also provides some nutritional benefits from the food, including vitamins and fiber.

Switching to a healthful diet does not mean sacrificing taste but rather replacing refined sugars with more natural sugars and sweet fruits. The recipes in this book do just that, providing a varied selection of wholesome dishes that are delicious too!

## SERVES 6-8

# GOLDEN RAISIN SODA BREAD

*Golden raisins add a natural sweetness which makes this bread ideal for
serving as a tea-time treat.*

1lb all-purpose white flour
1¼ tsps salt
1¼ tsps baking soda
1¼ tsps cream of tartar
1⅓ cups sour milk
⅔ cup golden raisins

**1.** Sift together the flour, salt, baking soda and cream of tartar in a mixing bowl.

**2.** Add the golden raisins and mix into the flour quickly, making a slight well in the center of the flour as you do so.

**3.** Pour the milk into the well in the flour, and mix with a round bladed knife to form a firm, but not too stiff dough.

**4.** Turn the dough onto a lightly floured board, and knead quickly to bring all the ingredients together well.

**5.** Shape the dough into a round, and flatten it slightly with the palm of your hand.

**6.** Place the dough round on a lightly greased and floured cookie sheet. Cut a deep cross into the top of the dough with a sharp knife.

**7.** Bake the dough in a preheated oven 400°F for 25 minutes.

**8.** After this time, turn the loaf upside down on the cookie sheet and return to the oven for a further 10 minutes to dry out completely.

**9.** Wrap the baked loaf in a damp cloth, and place on a wire rack to cool completely.

**Step 6** Cut a deep cross into the top of the bread dough using a sharp knife.

**Step 8** Turn the loaf upside down on the cookie sheet before returning to the oven for a further 10 minutes.

## Cook's Notes

**Time**
Preparation takes 15 minutes, cooking takes 35 minutes.

**Variation**
Use whole-wheat flour instead of the white flour in this recipe.

**Preparation**
To test that the loaf is completely cooked, tap the base with your fingers and if it sounds hollow it is ready.

**Cook's Tip**
If you do not have sour milk, use fresh milk with 1 tbsp of natural yogurt added.

**Freezing**
This bread freezes well.

MAKES 10-12

# RICH FRUIT BISCUITS

*Fruit biscuits are always a firm favorite and do not need any added sugar when made with plenty of fruit.*

½lb all-purpose flour
1¼ tsps cream of tartar
¾ tsp baking soda
⅓ tsp salt
3 tbsps butter
½ cup golden raisins
¾ tbsp sunflower seeds
½oz fresh stem ginger
2 eggs
Extra milk for blending
Beaten egg, for glaze

**Step 9** Roll out the dough to no less than ½-inch thick.

**Step 2** Rub the butter into the sieved flour until the mixture resembles fine breadcrumbs.

**1.** Mix the flour, cream of tartar, baking soda and salt together, and sieve it twice through a metal sieve to aerate completely.

**2.** Put the sieved flour into a large bowl, and rub in the butter until the mixture resembles fine breadcrumbs.

**3.** Stir the golden raisins and the sunflower seeds into the flour and butter mixture.

**4.** Peel the ginger, and cut or grate it into very small pieces.

**5.** Using a pestle and mortar or the handle of a large knife, crush the ginger until it becomes a paste.

**6.** Put the ginger into a small bowl along with the eggs, and beat together with a fork until they are evenly blended.

**7.** Add the beaten eggs and ginger to the flour and raisin mixture, mixing well to form a soft dough, and adding a little extra milk if the dough is too stiff.

**8.** Lightly flour a work surface. Turn out the dough and knead it lightly until it becomes smooth.

**9.** Roll the dough out to approximately ½-inch thick.

**10.** Cut the dough into 2-inch rounds using a biscuit cutter.

**11.** Place the biscuits on a greased cookie sheet, and brush each one with the extra beaten egg. Bake in a preheated oven 400°F for 10-15 minutes, or until golden brown and well risen.

## Cook's Notes

**Time**
Preparation takes approximately 15 minutes, cooking takes 10-15 minutes.

**Preparation**
Do not roll the dough out too thinly, otherwise the biscuits will not rise properly.

**Variation**
Use other combinations of dried fruit and nuts, or seeds, in place of the golden raisins and sunflower seeds in this recipe.

SERVES 6-8

# SUGAR-FREE FRUIT CAKE

*There is no need for sugar in a recipe rich in the natural sweetness of dried fruits.*

¼lbs all-purpose flour
¾ tsp baking soda
1¼ tsps mixed spice
1¼ tsps ground nutmeg
1 cup butter
2 cups raisins
1⅓ cups currants
2 cups golden raisins
⅔ cup mixed peel
1¼ cups Guinness, or stout
3 eggs

**Step 9** The cake batter should drop easily into the prepared pan, but not be too runny, or it will seep around the lining paper.

**1.** Sift the flour, baking soda, mixed spice and nutmeg into a large bowl, using a metal sieve.

**2.** Cut the butter into small dice, and rub into the flour using the fingertips, until the mixture resembles fine breadcrumbs.

**3.** Add all the fruit to the flour and mix well to distribute evenly.

**4.** Push the flour and fruit mixture away from the center of the bowl to form a slight well.

**5.** Put the Guinness and the eggs into a large jug and whisk together thoroughly, until frothy.

**6.** Pour the Guinness and eggs into the well in the center of the flour mixture.

**7.** Mix the Guinness and eggs together to form a soft batter, using a round bladed knife.

**8.** Grease and line a 9-inch round cake pan with wax paper.

**9.** Pour the cake batter into the pan and bake in the center of a preheated oven 325°F for 2 hours. Reduce the temperature to 275°F after the first hour if the cake appears to be cooking too quickly.

**10.** Test the cake with a skewer to see when it is done. If it is cooked, the skewer will come out clean. Turn the cake onto a wire rack, remove the lining paper and cool it completely before storing in an airtight tin for 2-3 days, before serving.

## Cook's Notes

**Time**
Preparation takes approximately 30 minutes, cooking takes 2 hours.

**Variation**
Use whole-wheat flour in place of the white flour in this recipe, cider instead of Guinness, and grated apple instead of mixed peel.

**Preparation**
If the cake is cooking too quickly, the sides will become brown and the center of the cake will rise up into a point. If this should happen, reduce the temperature and cook at a much slower heat. Cover the top of the cake with aluminium foil to prevent it from browning further.

**Cook's Tip**
The flavor of this cake really does improve if it can be kept in an airtight container for a few days before using.

**Freezing**
This cake freezes very well for up to 3 months.

# SERVES 4-6
# GRIDDLE SCONES

*The whole fun of these cakes is that they can be eaten directly from the pan in which they are cooked. So gather family and friends around you for a traditional tea-time treat.*

1 cup self-rising flour
Pinch salt
3 tbsps butter or margarine
⅔ cup currants
¾ tsp ground nutmeg
1 egg
⅓ cup milk

**Step 1** Rub the butter into the flour with your fingertips, until the mixture resembles fine breadcrumbs.

**Step 4** Using a wooden spoon, mix the egg and flour mixture into the flour, stirring from the center of the bowl and drawing the flour in from the sides to form a smooth, thick batter.

**Step 6** Fry tablespoons of the batter in a hot pan until the undersides have browned lightly and the tops are just set.

**1.** Mix the flour and salt together, and rub in the butter until the mixture resembles fine breadcrumbs.

**2.** Stir in the currants and the nutmeg, then push the mixture gently to the sides of the bowl to form a well in the center.

**3.** Beat together the egg and the milk, and pour the into the well in the center of the flour.

**4.** Using a wooden spoon, mix the egg and milk mixture into the flour, stirring from the center of the bowl and drawing the flour in from the sides to form a smooth, thick batter.

**5.** Heat a heavy-based frying pan on top of a moderate heat, and grease with a little butter or oil.

**6.** Drop tablespoons of the batter into the hot pan, and cook for 2-3 minutes, or until the bases are set and have turned golden brown.

**7.** Turn the scones over and cook on the other side in the same way.

**8.** Serve from the pan with sugar-free preserves.

## Cook's Notes

**Time**
Preparation takes 15 minutes, cooking takes about 4 minutes per scone.

**Preparation**
If the batter is too thick, add a little extra milk until it becomes a soft dropping consistency.

**Freezing**
These scones freeze well, and can be re-heated by wrapping in a clean dish towel and standing in a warm oven until they are heated through.

SERVES 6-8

# FRUIT LOAF

*There is no need to add sugar to this recipe as the easy-blend yeast will work on the natural sugars provided by the fruit.*

1lb all-purpose flour
¾ tsp cinnamon
¾ tsp nutmeg
¾ tsp salt
1⅓ cups golden raisins
1⅓ cups currants
⅓ cup cut mixed peel
1 package of easy blend yeast
2½ tbsps vegetable oil
1¼ cups lukewarm milk
1 large egg

**Step 4** Mix the milk mixture into the flour and yeast mixture, stirring until a soft, but elastic, dough is formed.

**Step 10** Shape the pieces of dough to fit into 2 lightly greased, or non-stick loaf pans.

**1.** Put the flour, spices and salt into a large mixing bowl.

**2.** Stir in the golden raisins, currants and mixed peel, mixing well to distribute the fruit evenly.

**3.** Sprinkle over the yeast, and mix this directly into the dry ingredients.

**4.** Put the oil, milk and egg into a large jug, and beat together with a fork until the egg is broken up evenly. Add the mixture to the flour, and mix together, stirring until the batter becomes stiff and elastic.

**5.** Turn the batter onto a lightly floured board, and knead until smooth – approximately 10 minutes.

**6.** Return the batter to the bowl and cover with a damp cloth or a piece of plastic wrap. Leave the batter in a warm place for about 1 hour to allow the dough to rise.

**7.** After this time, the dough should be approximately double its original size.

**8.** Punch the dough down to remove the air, and turn it out once again onto the lightly floured surface.

**9.** Continue kneading the dough for approximately 5 minutes, then cut in two.

**10.** Shape each piece of dough to fit 2 x 7-inch non-stick loaf pans. Cover each pan lightly with plastic wrap or a damp cloth, and leave once again in a warm place until the loaves have risen to double their size.

**11.** Bake the loaves for 30-40 minutes in the center of a preheated oven 400°F, removing the loaves from the oven after 20 minutes, and brushing the surfaces with a little milk.

**12.** To test if the loaves are cooked, turn out of the pans and tap the bases with your knuckles, if it sounds hollow, the loaves are ready.

**13.** Serve warm, or allow to cool and serve sliced, with butter.

## Cook's Notes

**Time**
Preparation takes approximately 2 hours, cooking takes 40 minutes.

**Variation**
Use any combination of your favorite dried fruits in this recipe.

**Freezing**
This recipe freezes well for up to 2 months.

MAKES 10

# FRUIT TRUFFLES

*These delicious little cakes get all the sweetness they require from fresh bananas.*

2 bananas
Juice ½ orange
Finely grated rind 1 orange
1¼ cups ground almonds
¼ cup blanched almonds
1¼ tbsps plain cocoa

**1.** Chop the bananas into a large bowl and using a potato masher, mash them until they are smooth.

**2.** Mix in the orange juice and rind.

**3.** Stir in the ground almonds, mixing well to blend evenly. Place the mixture in a refrigerator and chill for approximately 30 minutes.

**4.** Using a sharp knife, finely chop the blanched almonds into small pieces.

**5.** Mix the chopped almonds into the cocoa powder, and place on a flat plate.

**Step 1** Mash the bananas to a smooth pulp using a potato masher.

**Step 7** Roll the banana mixture into 10 even-sized balls, using lightly floured hands.

**Step 8** Cover each banana truffle with an even coating of chopped nuts and cocoa, pressing this gently onto the surface to ensure it stays in place.

**6.** Remove the banana mixture from the refrigerator, and divide into 10 portions.

**7.** Roll each portion into a small ball, using lightly floured hands.

**8.** Roll each ball into the cocoa and almond mixture, rolling each one evenly to give a good coating. Press gently before placing into a small paper cases, and chilling once again.

## Cook's Notes

**Time**
Preparation takes approximately 25 minutes, plus chilling time.

**Cook's Tip**
Do not keep these delicious sweets for long after they have been made, or the banana will go brown and wet.

**Variation**
Use walnuts in place of almonds in this recipe.

MAKES 2lbs

# COCONUT RELISH

*This unusual relish is a welcome change from the more common fruit relishes.*

2 fresh coconuts
½-inch piece fresh root ginger
2 green chilies
1¼ tsps cumin seed
5 tbsps finely chopped fresh coriander leaves
3¾ tbsps lemon juice
¾ tsp salt

**1.** Crack the coconuts in half, and carefully pour out and reserve the milk.

**2.** Remove the coconut flesh from inside the shells, and peel off the brown outer skin.

**3.** Chop the peeled coconut into small pieces.

**4.** Peel the root ginger and finely chop or grate the flesh.

**5.** Cut the green chilies in half, remove and discard the seeds, and finely chop the outer flesh.

**6.** Put the coconut, ginger, chilies, cumin seeds, coriander, lemon and salt into a liquidizer or food processor, and blend with enough coconut milk to produce a thick creamy relish.

**7.** Pour the mixture into pots and seal well.

**8.** Keep in a refrigerator and use within 2-3 weeks.

**Step 4** Finely chop or grate the peeled root ginger.

**Step 2** Peel away the brown skin from the flesh of the coconut using a sharp knife.

**Step 6** Blend the relish ingredients with coconut milk in a liquidizer or food processor until it is thick and creamy.

## Cook's Notes

**Time**
Preparation takes approximately 20 minutes.

**Freezing**
This recipe freezes well.

**Preparation**
If you do not have a liquidizer or a food processor, the coconut and other ingredients can be grated, but this will not produce such a smooth textured relish.

**Serving Idea**
This relish is delicious served with cold meats, curries, or in sandwiches.

MAKES APPROXIMATELY 5lbs

# FRUIT CHUTNEY

*The use of canned fruit means that this delicious chutney can be prepared at any time of the year.*

15oz can pears in natural juice
15oz can peach slices in natural juice
12oz can pineapple chunks in natural juice
8oz can prunes in natural juice
1lb plums
4 cooking apples
½ cup fresh dates, pitted
½ cup ready-to-use dried apricots
1-inch piece fresh root ginger, peeled and thinly sliced
1 cup blanched almonds
1 cup cashew nuts
5 tbsps malt vinegar
¾ tsp ground cloves
1¼ tsps chili powder
2-inch piece cinnamon stick
2 bananas, peeled and sliced

**1.** Remove the stones from the plums and chop the flesh into fairly large pieces.

**2.** Drain the fruit juices from the cans of fruit, and set aside. Chop the fruit into large pieces.

**3.** Cut the apples into four and remove the cores, but do not peel.

**4.** Finely slice the apple and mix this with the chopped fruit in a large saucepan.

**5.** Chop the dates and the dried apricots into small pieces. Add the apricots and dates to the saucepan of fruit, along with all the remaining ingredients, except for the reserved juice.

**6.** Pour over enough of the reserved juice to just cover the fruit.

**7.** Cover the pan, and bring the chutney to the boil. Reduce the heat and simmer for 15-20 minutes.

**8.** Remove the lid of the pan and stir the chutney well. Add a little extra juice if required, and continue cooking for a further 10 minutes, uncovered, stirring occasionally to prevent the mixture from burning.

**9.** When the chutney is thick and most of the liquid has evaporated, divide it between clean warm glass jars. Cover with waxed paper and a tight fitting lid, then store for up to 3 months in a refrigerator.

**Step 1** Cut the plums in half and carefully remove the stones. Chop the flesh into fairly large pieces.

**Step 9** When cooked, the chutney should be thick and most of the liquid should have evaporated.

## Cook's Notes

 **Time**
Preparation takes approximately 15 minutes, cooking takes 30 minutes.

 **Serving Idea**
Serve with cold meats, cheeses, or in sandwiches.

 **Cook's Tip**
Check that the chutney does not stick to the base of the pan, by stirring occasionally whilst it is cooking.

 **Variation**
If you cannot get fresh plums, try using mangoes or apricots.

 **Freezing**
This recipe will freeze well.

MAKES APPROXIMATELY 2lbs

# SUGAR-FREE MINCEMEAT

*Not only is this recipe free from refined sugar, it is also completely fat free, making it extremely healthful.*

3 large red eating apples
1⅓ cups raisins
1⅓ cups currants
1⅓ cups golden raisins
⅔ cup fresh dates
½ cup blanched almonds
⅔ cup brandy or sherry

**Step 3** Blend the pitted dates with the nuts and brandy, or sherry, until they are fairly coarsely chopped.

**Step 1** Quarter the apples, remove the cores and chop the flesh roughly.

**Step 4** Mix the date mixture with the apple and fruit mixture, stirring well to blend evenly.

**1.** Quarter the apples, remove the cores and chop the apple flesh.

**2.** Put the apples into a liquidizer or food processor, along with the raisins, currants and golden raisins. Chop the fruit finely, then transfer to a large mixing bowl.

**3.** Carefully remove the stones from the dates and put the fruit into a food processor or liquidizer, along with the nuts

and the brandy or sherry. Process until the dates and nuts are roughly chopped.

**4.** Mix the date mixture into the apple and dried fruit mixture, stirring well to blend all ingredients thoroughly.

**5.** Divide the mixture between 2-3 clean glass jars, then cover and allow to stand for up to 3 weeks before using.

## Cook's Notes

**Time**
Preparation takes approximately 20 minutes.

**Serving Idea**
Use in minced pies or apple pie as a natural sweetener.

**Freezing**
This recipe will freeze, but should be stirred well when thawed to distribute the alcohol evenly.

MAKES 2 cups

# CHOCOLATE BUTTER SAUCE

*The sugar-free (diabetic) chocolate used in this recipe is readily available in most health food shops.*

1 cup water
2 cups sugar-free chocolate, chopped
½ cup butter, cut into small pieces
1¼ tbsps brandy

**Step 1** Melt the chocolate in the water over a low heat, stirring until the mixture is smooth.

**1.** Put the water and the chocolate into a saucepan, and heat over a low heat, stirring until the chocolate has melted.

**2.** Remove the melted chocolate and water from the heat and slowly stir in the butter, piece by piece, until the mixture becomes thick and glossy.

**3.** Whisk the brandy into the butter sauce and spoon into an attractive serving dish. This sauce can be served hot or cold.

**Step 2** Drop the butter into the melted chocolate, piece by piece, stirring well until it has melted.

**Step 3** Beat the brandy into the sauce, whisking until it is thick and glossy.

## Cook's Notes

 **Time**
Preparation takes approximately 5 minutes, cooking takes 10 minutes.

 **Preparation**
After melting the chocolate and water together, the mixture should be smooth, with no lumps in it.

 **Serving Idea**
Serve with fresh fruit or pancakes.

 **Watchpoint**
Do not heat the chocolate and water too rapidly or the mixture will curdle.

MAKES 1 cup

# MOCHA SAUCE

*This unusual coffee chocolate sauce gets its sweetness from the delightfully tangy apricot purée.*

1 cup sugar-free chocolate
3¾ tbsps very strong black coffee
½ cup heavy cream
½ cup thick apricot purée (see separate recipe)

**Step 3** Stir the heavy cream into the chocolate and coffee mixture, mixing well to blend evenly.

**Step 2** Melt the chocolate and coffee together in a bowl which is standing over a saucepan of hot water.

**1.** Grate the chocolate, or chop it into small pieces with a sharp knife.

**2.** Put the chocolate and the coffee into a large bowl, and stand the bowl over a saucepan half filled with simmering water. Remove the saucepan and the bowl from the heat, and stir the chocolate gently until it has melted.

**3.** Add the heavy cream to the melted chocolate, mixing well to blend evenly.

**4.** Stir in the apricot purée, transfer the chocolate sauce to a serving dish and chill thoroughly.

## Cook's Notes

 **Time**
Preparation takes approximately 5 minutes, cooking takes 15 minutes.

 **Serving Idea**
Serve this delicious sauce with fruit or pancakes.

 **Watchpoint**
Take great care not to cook the chocolate and the coffee together too quickly, or the chocolate will separate and curdle.

MAKES APPROXIMATELY 1½ cups

# APRICOT PURÉE

*This delicious tangy sauce is made with canned apricots in natural juice,*
*thus making use of the natural sweetness of fruit sugars.*

15oz can apricot halves in natural juice
Juice and rind 1 lime
2½ tbsps apricot brandy (optional)

**1.** Purée the apricots in their juice, using a liquidizer or food processor.

**2.** Put the apricot purée into a small saucepan.

**3.** Stir the lime juice and rind into the apricot mixture, and heat over a low temperature until it begins to boil.

**4.** Continue simmering over a low temperature until the sauce is thick and liquid has reduced.

**Step 1** Purée the apricots in a liquidizer or food processor until they are smooth.

**Step 3** Stir the lime juice and rind into the fruit purée, mixing well to blend evenly.

**Step 4** Cook the apricot mixture over a low heat until the sauce has thickened and the liquid has evaporated.

**5.** Cool the purée in a refrigerator until required, and serve after stirring in the apricot brandy.

---

## Cook's Notes

**Time**
Preparation takes 2 minutes, cooking takes 5 minutes.

**Variation**
Use canned pears or prunes in place of the apricots in this recipe.

**Serving Idea**
Serve with pancakes, or fresh fruit.

---

SERVES 10-12

# APPLE SAUCE

*This sauce is extremely versatile and can be used as an accompaniment to meats or fish, as well as being included in ingredients for desserts.*

2lbs cooking apples
1¼ cups apple juice
⅓ tsp ground cloves
Finely pared rind ½ orange

**1.** Wash the apples and cut away any bruised or discolored pieces. Cut the fruit into large pieces.

**2.** Put the chopped fruit into a large pan, along with the apple juice, ground cloves and the orange rind. Bring to the boil and simmer until most of the liquid has evaporated and the fruit has softened.

**3.** Cool the cooked apples.

**4.** Put the cooled apples into a nylon sieve over a large bowl, and press through using the back of a wooden spoon, to remove all skin, pips and cores.

**5.** Put the apple purée into cartons or jars, and store or freeze until required.

**6.** Serve in a bowl and decorate with a sprig of mint.

**Step 1** Wash the apples and cut away any bruising or discolored pieces.

**Step 2** Cook the apples in the fruit juice until the liquid has reduced, and the fruit is soft and pulpy.

**Step 4** Press the cooled fruit through a nylon sieve into a bowl, using the back of a wooden spoon to push the fruit purée through and to remove the cores, skin and pips.

## Cook's Notes

**Time**
Preparation takes approximately 30 minutes, cooking takes about 20 minutes.

**Preparation**
If preferred, the cooked apples can be puréed in a liquidizer or food processor before pressing through the sieve to remove the skins and cores.

**Variation**
Use cinnamon instead of the cloves in this recipe.

**Freezing**
This sauce can be frozen for up to 4 months.

MAKES 10-12 PANCAKES

# CREPES

*These tasty pancakes are delicious with both sweet and tangy sauces.*

1 cup all-purpose flour
Pinch salt
1 egg
1¼ cups milk
1¼ tsps vegetable oil
Juice and rind of a lemon and orange

**1.** Sieve the flour and the salt into a large bowl. Push the flour gently towards the sides of the bowl to make a well in the center.

**2.** Put the egg and the milk into a jug and beat well.

**3.** Gradually add the egg and milk mixture to the flour, pouring it into the center of the bowl, and mixing gently by stirring and drawing the flour in from the sides.

**4.** Continue adding the egg mixture gradually and beat until all the flour has been incorporated.

**5.** Heat a little oil in a small frying pan, and pour in enough batter to make a thin pancake.

**6.** Quickly tilt and rotate the frying pan so that the batter coats the bottom of it evenly.

**7.** Cook the pancake over a moderate heat until the underside has turned brown and the top has set.

**8.** Carefully turn the pancake over and brown the other side in the same way.

**9.** Turn each pancake out onto wax paper and keep them warm until required.

**10.** Serve the pancakes hot with freshly squeezed orange and lemon juice and decorate with the pared citrus rind.

**Step 1** Gently push the flour towards the sides of the bowl to make a well in the center.

**Step 3** Gradually add the egg and milk to the flour, mixing from the center of the bowl and drawing the flour into the liquid.

**Step 6** Quickly tilt and rotate the frying pan so that the batter coats the bottom thinly.

## Cook's Notes

**Time**
Preparation takes approximately 10 minutes, cooking takes about 20 minutes for all the pancakes.

**Watchpoint**
Do not overheat your frying pan or the base of the pancake will burn before the top has set. Also, do not attempt to turn the pancakes until the underside is properly cooked.

**Freezing**
Pancakes can be made in greater quantities than this recipe, and frozen until required.

MAKES 2 x 2 PINT PUDDINGS

# PLUM PUDDING

*Plum puddings are always thought of as being sweet and heavy. Try this sugar-free recipe for a fresh tasting change.*

1lb mixed dried fruit
1 cup seedless raisins
1 cup pitted dates
1 cup pitted, ready to use prunes
½ cup blanched shredded almonds
3 cups fresh white breadcrumbs
⅔ cup shredded suet
1½ cups all-purpose flour
½ tsp ground nutmeg
¾ tsp ground cinnamon
¼ tsp salt
1 carrot, grated
1 cooking apple, grated
Grated rind and juice 1 orange
⅔ cup brandy, or stout
1 egg

**1.** Put all the fruit into a mincer or food processor and chop finely.

**2.** Put the chopped fruits into a large mixing bowl, add all the remaining ingredients, and mix well.

**Step 2** Mix the minced fruit together in a large bowl with all the remaining ingredients, stirring well to blend thoroughly.

**3.** Grease 2 x 2 pint pudding bowls, and divide the mixture evenly between both bowls.

**4.** Cover the top of the puddings with a buttered circle of wax paper.

**5.** Make a foil pudding lid by cutting a large piece of aluminum foil, and pleating it down the center. Tie this lid securely onto the bowls.

**6.** Stand the puddings on an up-turned saucer or trivet, in a large saucepan.

**7.** Add enough boiling water to the saucepans to come two thirds of the way up the side of the pudding bowls.

**8.** Cover the saucepans and boil the puddings for 4-5 hours, keeping the water topped up as it evaporates.

**9.** Remove the bowls from the water and remove the covering paper.

**10.** Up-turn a serving plate over the puddings, and turn the whole pudding over, shaking it gently to help it drop out of the bowl onto the serving plate.

**11.** Serve ignited with brandy, if desired.

**Step 5** Cover the pudding with a pleated foil pudding lid, tying this down securely before boiling.

## Cook's Notes

**Time**
Preparation takes approximately 30 minutes, cooking takes about 5 hours.

**Serving Idea**
Serve with brandy butter or fresh cream.

**Preparation**
To be at its best this pudding should be prepared at least 3 months in advance.

**Cook's Tip**
This pudding can be stored for up to a year. To re-heat before use, pop into a pan of simmering water and cook for 3 hours.

SERVES 4-6

# COCONUT SORBET

*Naturally sweet coconut milk and dark rum blend lusciously to produce a
sorbet rich with the flavors of the Caribbean.*

14oz can coconut milk
⅓ cup mineral water
⅓ cup dark rum
2 egg whites
Liquid sweetener to taste (optional)
2 bananas, thinly sliced and brushed with lemon juice
and flaked coconut, to decorate

**1.** Mix the coconut milk with the mineral water, rum and liquid sweetener to taste, if required. Pour into a large freezer container and put into the freezer for 1 hour, or until the sides are beginning to freeze.

**2.** Using a fork, break the frozen coconut mixture up into a thin slush, making sure that there are no large ice crystals left in the mixture. Return to the freezer and continue freezing for a further hour.

**3.** Remove the coconut mixture from the freezer, and break up as before with a fork to make a thicker slush. Return the mixture to the freezer whilst you whisk the egg whites.

**4.** Whisk the egg whites until they form soft peaks.

**5.** Remove the partially frozen coconut mixture from the freezer and make sure that it can be easily stirred.

**6.** Carefully fold the egg whites into the coconut mixture, mixing lightly but thoroughly to blend evenly.

**Step 2** Break the crystals away from the edge of the freezer dish using a fork, and mixing well to make a thin slush.

**Step 6** Fold the softly whipped egg whites into the partially frozen slush, mixing lightly but thoroughly, to blend evenly.

**7.** Return the sorbet to the freezer and freeze until completely set.

**8.** To serve, remove the sorbet from the freezer 10 minutes before it is required and break it up with a fork into large ice crystals. Pile the crystals into serving dishes and decorate with the banana and the flakes of coconut.

## Cook's Notes

**Time**
Preparation takes approximately 20 minutes, freezing takes 2-3 hours.

**Variation**
Use pineapple juice in place of the rum, and serve with pineapple pieces and coconut flakes.

**Preparation**
Make sure that the ice crystals are not too wet when you fold in the egg whites, otherwise the mixture will separate during freezing.

**Cook's Tip**
Make double quantities of this sorbet, as it freezes well for up to 3 months and is ideal as a stand-by dessert.

SERVES 4-6

# EXOTIC FRUIT SALAD

*Mangoes are exceptionally sweet when ripe, and give this lovely fruit salad a
natural tangy sweetness.*

3 ripe peaches
3 kiwi fruits
1 large star fruit
⅔ cup fresh strawberries
2 well-ripened mangoes, each weighing about 12oz
Juice of half a lime
1 cup redcurrants
Few strawberry leaves for decoration

**Step 9** Press the mango purée through a wire sieve, using a wooden spoon to remove the pips and skins from the redcurrants.

**Step 5** Cut away any brown pieces from the skin of the star fruit using a sharp knife.

**1.** Plunge the peaches into boiling water for a few seconds, then carefully peel away the skin using a sharp knife.

**2.** Carefully cut the peaches in half and remove the stone.

**3.** Cut the peach halves into thin slices and arrange on a serving plate.

**4.** Cut away the peel from the kiwi fruits and slice them crosswise to show their attractive color.

**5.** Trim away any dark pieces from the skin of the star fruit, cut the flesh into thin slices, and remove any small pips you may find.

**6.** Leave the green stems on the strawberries and cut them in half lengthways. Arrange all the prepared fruit on the serving platter with the peaches.

**7.** Peel the mango and chop away the flesh from the large inner stone.

**8.** Put the chopped mango flesh into a liquidizer or food processor, along with the lime juice and half of the redcurrants.

**9.** Purée the mixture until smooth, then press the purée through a nylon sieve to remove the redcurrant skins and pips.

**10.** Sprinkle the remaining redcurrants over the fruit on the serving platter, removing any hard stems or leaves as you do so.

**11.** Pour the fruit purée evenly over the fruit salad, and chill for at least 1 hour before serving, decorated with the strawberry leaves.

## Cook's Notes

**Time**
Preparation takes approximately 25 minutes, plus 1 hour chilling time.

**Variation**
Use any combination of your favorite fruits in the fruit salad, but do not change the mango purée.

**Preparation**
If you do not have a liquidizer or food processor, a really ripe mango will rub easily through a wire sieve and will not need to be reduced to a purée first.

**Cook's Tip**
Add 3 tbsps rum to the mango purée to give extra flavor for a special occasion.

# SERVES 6
# RASPBERRY SOUFFLÉ

*This light dessert is the perfect finale for a dinner party.*

1lb raspberries
Liquid sweetener to taste
2 tbsps gelatin
⅔ cup hot water
4 eggs, separated
1¼ cups heavy cream

**1.** Prepare a 6-inch souffle dish by tightly tying a lightly oiled sheet of wax paper carefully around the outside edge of the souffle dish, allowing it to stand approximately 4 inches above the rim of the dish.

**2.** Reserve a few of the raspberries for decoration, and purée the remainder using a liquidizer or food processor.

**3.** Rub the puréed raspberries through a nylon sieve to remove the hard pips.

**4.** Sweeten the smooth raspberry purée with the liquid sweetener and set aside.

**5.** Dissolve the gelatin in the hot water, stirring gently until it is completely dissolved and the liquid is clear.

**6.** Allow the gelatin to cool slightly and then beat it into the raspberry purée along with the egg yolks, mixing until all ingredients are well blended. Chill in the refrigerator until partially set.

**7.** Whisk the egg whites until they form soft peaks.

**8.** Lightly whip half of the heavy cream until it is softly stiff.

**9.** Remove the partially set raspberry mixture from the refrigerator, and carefully fold in the cream and the egg

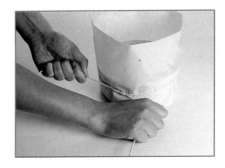

**Step 1** Tie a sheet of wax paper around the souffle dish, to form a collar rising above the rim of the dish.

**Step 3** Press the raspberry purée through a metal sieve, to remove the pips.

whites, blending lightly but thoroughly until the mixture is smooth.

**10.** Turn the prepared souffle mixture into the dish, allowing it to rise about 1 inch above the rim of the dish inside the paper collar. Allow to set in the refrigerator.

**11.** When completely set, remove the collar carefully and decorate the souffle with the remaining whipped cream and the reserved raspberries.

## Cook's Notes

**Time**
Preparation takes approximately 40 minutes, plus chilling time.

**Watchpoint**
Do not add the gelatin to boiling water, or this will impair its setting qualities.

**Preparation**
Take great care not to over-mix the souffle mixture when adding the egg whites, or there will not be enough to rise up over the rim of the dish inside the collar.

**Variation**
Use strawberries, or any other favorite fresh fruit in place of the raspberries in this recipe.

**Freezing**
Cold souffles freeze very well for up to 6 weeks, but should be decorated after they have thawed.

SERVES 4

# PASSION FRUIT ICE CREAM

*Fruit ice creams are actually more refreshing without added sugar, but if you must have added sweetness use liquid sweetener.*

6 passion fruits
1¼ cups natural yogurt
2 egg yolks
Liquid sweetener to taste (optional)
1-2 passion fruits, halved and scooped for decoration

**Step 1** Cut the 6 passion fruits in half and scoop all the center pulp into a bowl using a small spoon.

**Step 2** Beat together the yogurt, egg yolks and passion fruit pulp until they are well blended.

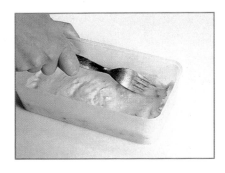

**Step 4** Break up the partially frozen passion fruit ice cream using a fork, and mixing until a smooth slush is formed.

**1.** Halve the 6 passion fruits, and scoop out all the center pulp into a bowl.

**2.** Add the yogurt and egg yolks to the passion fruit pulp, and mix together well, adding liquid sweetener to taste, if desired.

**3.** Pour the passion fruit mixture into a shallow container, and freeze until partially set – approximately 1 hour.

**4.** Break the ice crystals in the partially set passion fruit mixture using a fork, and mixing well until they form a smooth slush.

**5.** Return the ice cream to the freezer and freeze until completely firm.

**6.** To serve, remove the ice cream from the freezer for 10 minutes, then pile scoops of ice cream into stemmed glasses, and serve with passion fruit pulp poured over each portion.

## Cook's Notes

**Time**
Preparation takes approximately 20 minutes, plus freezing time.

**Variation**
Add 2 tbsps rum or brandy to the ice cream mixture before freezing.

**Watchpoint**
This ice cream goes extremely hard when frozen, so it is important to remember to remove it from the freezer 10 minutes before serving.

SERVES 4

# STUFFED FIGS

*Fresh figs are now easily available from most major supermarkets and good greengrocers. When ripe, they go a luscious purple black and are soft to the touch.*

4 large ripe figs
5 tbsps ground almonds
2½ tbsps orange juice
2½ tbsps finely chopped dried apricots
5 tbsps natural yogurt
Finely grated rind ½ orange
Wedges of figs and mint, or strawberry leaves for decoration

**Step 2** Ease the four sections of each fig outwards to form a flower shape.

**Step 1** Carefully cut a cross into each fig, making sure that you do not cut right through the base.

**Step 4** Divide the almond mixture evenly between the four figs, and press it into the center of each one.

**1.** Cut each fig into four quarters using a sharp knife, and taking care not to cut right down through the base.

**2.** Ease the four sections of each fig outward to form a flower shape.

**3.** Put the ground almonds, orange juice and chopped apricots into a small bowl and mix together thoroughly.

**4.** Divide this mixture into four, and press it into the center

of each fig.

**5.** For the sauce, mix the yogurt with the orange rind, and thin it down with just a little water, or orange juice.

**6.** Spoon a small pool of orange yogurt onto each of four plates, and sit a stuffed fig into the center of each pool. Decorate with the additional wedges of fig, and the mint or strawberry leaves.

## Cook's Notes

**Time**
Preparation takes approximately 25 minutes.

**Variation**
Use peach halves instead of the figs in this recipe.

**Watchpoint**
Do not add too much water or orange juice to the sauce, or it will become too thin.

SERVES 6

# CHERRIES IN SYRUP

*Black cherries and apple juice combine perfectly in this tasty dessert.*

1½lbs fresh black cherries
2 cups apple or grape juice
1¾ tsps finely grated lemon rind
3 tbsps cornstarch or arrowroot
3¾ tbsps brandy (optional)

**1.** Remove the stones from the cherries, using a cherry pitter or the rounded end of a potato peeler.

**2.** Put the pitted cherries into a saucepan, along with the apple or grape juice and the lemon rind. Bring to the boil over a moderate heat, then simmer for 10 minutes, or until the cherries are gently poached.

**3.** Remove the cherries from the juice with a slotted spoon, leaving the juice in the saucepan. Arrange the cherries in a serving bowl.

**4.** Blend the cornstarch with 5 tbsps of the cherry juice.

**5.** Add the blended cornstarch or arrowroot to the cherry juice in the pan, and bring to the boil stirring constantly until the sauce has thickened. Stir in the brandy if used.

**6.** Pour the thickened cherry sauce over the cherries in the bowl, and chill well before serving.

**Step 1** Remove the stones from the cherries using a cherry pitter or the rounded end of a potato peeler.

**Step 4** Blend cornstarch or arrowroot with 5 tbsps of the cherry juice.

**Step 5** Bring the cherry juice and blended cornstarch or arrowroot, slowly to the boil, stirring all the time until the sauce thickens and clears.

## Cook's Notes

**Time**
Preparation takes 15-20 minutes, cooking takes about 5 minutes plus chilling time.

**Cook's Tip**
Arrowroot will produce a clearer sauce than cornstarch.

**Variation**
Use apricots instead of cherries in this recipe.

**Freezing**
This recipe freezes well.

SERVES 4-6

# ORANGE AND APRICOT MOUSSE

*This delicious light mousse makes an ideal end to any meal.*

2 oranges
3 x 14oz cans of apricots in natural juice, drained
Artificial sweetener to taste (optional)
2 tbsps powdered gelatin
⅔ cup natural yogurt
2 egg whites
Extra orange rind to decorate

**1.** Finely grate the rind from half of one orange using a fine grater.

**2.** Cut all the oranges in half and squeeze out the juice.

**3.** Put the drained apricots, all but 3 tbsps of the orange juice, and the orange rind into a liquidizer or food processor, and purée until smooth. Pour into a large bowl and set aside.

**4.** Put the 3 tbsps of orange juice into a small pan and heat gently, but do not boil.

**5.** Sprinkle the gelatin over the warm orange juice, and allow to stand until dissolved and clear.

**6.** Stir the gelatin mixture into the apricot purée, along with the natural yogurt, mixing well to blend evenly. Put in a refrigerator for about 30 minutes until almost set.

**7.** Whisk the egg whites until they form soft peaks.

**8.** Fold the whisked egg whites lightly, but thoroughly, into the partially set apricot mixture.

**9.** Divide the fruit mousse evenly into serving glasses and chill until completely set.

**Step 3** Purée the orange juice, rind and apricots together in a liquidizer or food processor until smooth.

**Step 6** Allow the fruit purée and gelatin to chill in a refrigerator until it is just beginning to set.

**Step 8** Fold the egg whites carefully, but thoroughly, into the thickening fruit mixture, taking care not to over mix and lose the air in the egg whites.

## Cook's Notes

**Time**
Preparation takes 30-35 minutes, plus chilling time.

**Variation**
Use strawberries or peaches in place of the apricots.

**Serving Idea**
Serve decorated with twisted strips of orange peel and a crisp biscuit if liked.

SERVES 6

# BAKED APPLES IN PASTRY

*Pastry sweetened with cinnamon and spices combines with a rich fruit filling to make this warming winter dessert.*

3 cups all-purpose flour
¼ tsp salt
⅓ tsp cinnamon
⅓ tsp ground nutmeg
¾ cup butter
6-8 tbsps iced water
6 medium-sized dessert apples
6 prunes, pitted
6 dried apricots
2½ tbsps raisins
1 egg, beaten to glaze
Fresh cream to serve
Fresh mint to serve

**1.** Sift the flour, salt and spices into a large bowl.

**2.** Cut the butter into dice and rub into the flour until the mixture resembles fine breadcrumbs.

**3.** Mix in enough water to produce a smooth pliable dough.

**4.** Divide the dough into six pieces and roll out into a square approximately 8 inches.

**5.** Peel the apples with a sharp knife and carefully remove the center cores with an apple corer.

**6.** Chop the prunes and the apricots and mix these with the raisins.

**Step 8** Draw the sides of the pastry square up and over each apple, sealing the edges well with a little water.

**7.** Place one prepared apple into the center of each pastry square, and fill the cavities with equal amounts of the dried fruit mixture.

**8.** Brush the edges of each square with a little water, and draw them up and around the sides of the apples, sealing them well with a little water and trimming off any excess pastry to give a neat finish.

**9.** Roll out the pastry trimmings, cut into decorative leaves and stick the leaves onto each apple for decoration.

**10.** Glaze each pastry apple with the beaten egg and place on a lightly greased cookie sheet.

**11.** Bake the apples in a preheated oven 350°F for 20-25 minutes, or until golden brown.

**12.** Serve hot with the fresh cream and sprigs of fresh mint.

## Cook's Notes

**Time**
Preparation takes approximately 30 minutes, cooking time takes 20-25 minutes.

**Cook's Tip**
For an extra rich pastry, use 1 egg yolk and half the amount of water in this recipe.

**Variation**
Use pears instead of apples in this recipe.

**Freezing**
These apples freeze well after baking and should be thawed, then re-heated, before eating.

## SERVES 6

# ALMOND-YOGURT SHAKE

*This healthy, sugar-free yogurt shake has a slightly salty,*
*but refreshing flavor.*

1¾ cups water
2 cups natural yogurt
2½ tsps lemon juice
2½ tbsps ground almonds
¼ tsp saffron strands
2½ tsps rose water
¼ tsp salt

**1.** Lightly moisten the rims of six tumblers with a little water or lightly whipped egg white. Spread a thin layer of salt onto a saucer and dip the moistened rims into it to coat lightly.

**2.** Put half of the water into a liquidizer and add the yogurt, lemon juice, almonds, saffron and rose water. Blend until smooth.

**3.** Mix in the remaining water and the salt.

**Step 1** Lightly moisten the rims of six tumblers with a little water or lightly whipped egg white. Spread a thin layer of salt onto a saucer and dip the moistened rims into it to coat lightly.

**4.** Measure 1 pint of ice cubes into a measuring jug.

**5.** Pour the yogurt mixture from the liquidizer into another large jug.

**6.** Put half of the ice into the liquidizer and pour over half of the yogurt and saffron mixture. Blend to a thick slush, then repeat with the remaining ice and yogurt mixture. Serve in the prepared tumblers.

**Step 2** Blend the water, yogurt, lemon juice, almonds, saffron and rose water in a liquidizer or food processor, until smooth.

**Step 6** Blend half of the ice with half of the liquid in the liquidizer until it forms a smooth slush.

## Cook's Notes

**Time**
Preparation takes 10 minutes.

**Cook's Tip**
If you haven't got a liquidizer or food processor, use a rolling pin to crush the ice.

**Variation**
Use the juice of ½ an orange in place of the lemon juice in this recipe.

## SERVES 6

# KIWI AND PINEAPPLE SHAKE

*Sugar-free lemonade is easily available in supermarkets, and adds a tangy fizz to this delicious fruity drink.*

1 cup pineapple juice
3 kiwi fruits
1¼ cups natural yogurt
1 lemon
Liquid sweetener to taste
2 cups ice cubes
1¼ cups sugar-free lemonade
1 kiwi fruit for decoration

**Step 1** Purée the pineapple juice and kiwi fruits together in a liquidizer or food processor, until smooth.

**1.** Carefully peel the 3 kiwi fruits and roughly chop the flesh. Put the kiwi flesh into a food processor or liquidizer, along with the pineapple juice, and blend until smooth.

**2.** Finely grate the rind from half of the lemon and squeeze the juice. Mix the juice into the yogurt in a large jug, along with the fruit purée and liquid sweetener.

**3.** Put the ice cubes into the food processor or liquidizer, and pour over the pineapple and yogurt mixture. Blend for

15-30 seconds until it becomes a smooth slush.

**4.** Divide this mixture between six glasses and top up with lemonade, stirring well with a long handled spoon to blend in the glass.

**5.** Cut the unpeeled kiwi fruit into thin slices and slit each slice halfway through. Stand each slice of kiwi onto the sides of each glass for decoration.

**Step 2** Blend the yogurt, lemon rind and juice, liquid sweetener, and the pineapple and kiwi fruit mixture together in a large jug.

**Step 3** Blend together the ice and the pineapple yogurt mixture until it becomes a smooth slush.

## Cook's Notes

**Time**
Preparation takes 5-10 minutes.

**Cook's Tip**
Do not use set yogurt in this drink as it will not blend smoothly.

**Variation**
Use orange juice in place of the pineapple juice in this recipe.

SERVES 4

# TROPICAL FRUIT HEALTH DRINK

*This healthful fruit drink is an ideal breakfast time treat.*

3 kiwi fruits
2 ripe nectarines or peaches
2 slices fresh pineapple
1 lime
1¼ cups unsweetened pineapple juice
1 kiwi fruit or lime, for decoration

**Step 5** Blend the fruit and the juices in a liquidizer or food processor, until smooth.

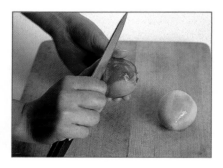

**Step 2** Carefully peel away the skin from the blanched nectarines or peaches, using a sharp knife.

**Step 3** Cut the peaches in half and twist them carefully apart to remove the stones.

**1.** Carefully remove the peel from the kiwi fruit and roughly chop the flesh.

**2.** Plunge the nectarines or peaches into boiling water for 30 seconds and carefully peel off the blanched skins.

**3.** Halve the peaches or nectarines, and remove the stones. Chop the flesh and put this into a liquidizer or food processor, along with the kiwi fruit.

**4.** Remove the peel from the pineapple slices and cut into quarters. Cut away the tough core from the pineapple and add the remaining flesh to the kiwi and peaches in the liquidizer or food processor.

**5.** Squeeze the juice from the lime and add this, with the pineapple juice, to the fruit in the food processor. Blend until smooth, and pour into individual serving glasses.

**6.** Decorate the edge of the glasses with thin slices of un-peeled kiwi fruit or lime.

## Cook's Notes

**Time**
Preparation takes approximately 10 minutes.

**Variation**
Add 1¼ cups sugar-free lemonade to this recipe for a lighter more refreshing fruit drink.

**Serving Idea**
Serve spooned over muesli for a refreshing breakfast.

SERVES 4-6

# SPICED MANGO JUICE

*Fresh mango juice is not easily available in shops, but is so easy to make that it is well worth producing your own.*

3 large ripe mangoes
⅔ tsp ground ginger
⅔ tsp ground cinnamon
1¼ cups unsweetened orange juice
1 lemon
1 orange for decoration

**1.** Peel the mangoes and cut the flesh away from the stone.

**2.** Put the mango flesh into a liquidizer or food processor along with the spices and orange juice. Blend until smooth.

**3.** Cut the lemon in half and squeeze the juice.

**4.** Add enough lemon juice to the mango purée to suit your own preference.

**5.** Pour the mango juice into individual serving glasses.

**6.** Slice the orange thinly and use these to decorate the sides of the glass.

**Step 1** Carefully cut away the mango flesh from the long inside stone using a sharp knife.

**Step 2** Blend the fruit, spices and orange juice together in a liquidizer or food processor, until they are smooth.

## Cook's Notes

**Time**
Preparation takes about 15 minutes.

**Cook's Tip**
Use this drink, mixed with ½ cup dark rum for an unusual cocktail.

**Variation**
Add 1 large peeled banana to the mango mixture before puréeing for a thicker, and more filling breakfast drink.

SERVES 6-8

# CARDAMOM-
# SPICED COFFEE

*This rich spicy flavored coffee is a traditional drink in Arabian countries.*

4½ cups water
1¾ cups milk
2½ tbsps fresh ground roast coffee
Seeds of 4 small cardamoms, crushed

**Step 3** Crush the cardamom seeds in a pestle and mortar until they are fine.

**Step 2** Add the coffee to the boiled water and milk, and mix well.

**Step 4** Strain the coffee mixture through a metal sieve to remove the ground cardamom seeds.

**1.** Put the water and milk into a saucepan and bring to the boil.

**2.** Add the coffee and mix well.

**3.** Crush the cardamom seeds finely using a pestle and mortar. Stir into the coffee and liquid in the saucepan. Cover the pan and remove from the heat. Allow to stand for 2-3 minutes.

**4.** Strain the coffee mixture through a metal sieve into cups and serve straight away.

## Cook's Notes

**Time**
Preparation takes about 8 minutes.

**Cook's Tip**
If you have a coffee grinder, grind the coffee beans yourself for a really fresh flavor.

**Variation**
Omit the cardamoms from this recipe if preferred.

SERVES 6

# ORANGE-SPICED TEA

*A deliciously different way of serving tea, this recipe is refreshing served either hot or cold.*

4½ cups water
½-inch piece cinnamon stick
4 cloves
Seeds of 4 cardamoms
3 strips of orange peel
2½ tbsps tea leaves
Milk to taste

**1.** Put the cinnamon, cloves and cardamom seeds into a pestle and mortar and crush roughly.

**2.** Put the water into a large saucepan with the orange peel and bring to the boil.

**3.** Remove the saucepan from the heat and add the spices and tea leaves. Allow to infuse for 2-3 minutes, keeping the pan covered.

**4.** Strain the tea through a fine tea strainer into cups, and serve with milk if preferred, or black with a sprig of mint.

**Step 2** Bring the water and orange peel to the boil.

**Step 1** Crush the cinnamon, cloves and cardamom seeds roughly in a pestle and mortar.

**Step 4** Strain the infused tea into cups through a fine tea strainer to remove the tea leaves and flavorings.

## Cook's Notes

**Time**
Preparation takes 10-15 minutes.

SERVES 4

# GRAPEFRUIT CUP

*Ruby grapefruits give this delicious refreshing drink a lovely color as well as a natural sweetness.*

2 ruby grapefruits
1¼ cups unsweetened grapefruit juice, preferably ruby
½ cup water
2 egg whites
Small sprigs of fresh mint to decorate

1. Carefully cut the peel from around the grapefruits, removing all the white pith as you go.

2. Cut the grapefruits into segments by carefully slicing between the flesh and the thin inner membranes.

3. Put the grapefruit segments, grapefruit juice, and the water into a liquidizer or food processor, and blend until smooth.

4. Add the egg whites to the grapefruit mixture and blend once again until it becomes frothy.

5. Pour the drink into glasses, making sure that a good portion of the white froth goes into each one.

6. Decorate with the sprigs of mint and serve immediately.

**Step 1** Carefully cut away all the peel and the pith from each grapefruit, using a sharp knife.

**Step 2** Cut the grapefruit segments away from the thin inner membranes using a sharp knife.

## Cook's Notes

**Time**
Preparation takes 10-15 minutes.

**Preparation**
Squeeze all the juice from the discarded membrane into the liquidizer before blending.

**Cook's Tip**
For a speedy method of preparing this drink, use a can of unsweetened grapefruit segments in place of the fresh fruit in this recipe.

**Variation**
Use normal grapefruits or sweet grapefruits for a variation in flavor.

# Index

**COMPILED BY PATRICIA PAYNE**
**EDITED BY JILLIAN STEWART**
**PHOTOGRAPHY BY PETER BARRY**
**RECIPES STYLED BY HELEN BURDETT**
**DESIGNED BY SALLY STRUGNELL**
**COVER DESIGN BY MARILYN O'NEONS**